Little Creatures

An Introduction to Classical Music

Music selection and explanatory notes **Ana Gerhard** Illustrations **Mauricio Gómez Morin**

Little Creatures

We often refer to insects, the largest and most diverse group of animals on the planet, as bugs, a term we also use for microbes. Amphibians and reptiles may occasionally be labelled vermin (a term also applied to some human lowlifes!). In short, we disdain any creature whose unpleasant or alarming appearance gives rise to an uneasy feeling or revulsion.

In this book, we have brought together twenty musical compositions by musicians who were drawn to animals that seldom get much attention.

You will discover melodies inspired by creatures as small as a flea or as large as a snake, by flying insects such as honeybees, wasps, butterflies and bumblebees, and by jumping animals the likes of crickets, frogs and grasshoppers.

In some cases, the composer imitated the creature's sound. Some of these little creatures can make quite a racket and put on a show when they get together for an all-night party, carrying on and playing while the children sleep!

In other cases, the composer employs a variety of musical resources to evoke a creature's movement: the voices of a full choir suggesting flies buzzing about, a harpsichord melody with ever-wider intervals depicting the acrobatics of a flea, or the constant alternation of two notes to portray the sinister slithering of a snake.

The works selected for this musical picture book cover five centuries and come from a variety of musical traditions. Despite their diversity, they have one thing in common: they invite the listener to stop and notice the little creatures around us. When we turn our attention to even the smallest and most insignificant of beings, we can find beautiful music in them. We hope you will accept that invitation.

1 The Tale of Tsar Saltan

Flight of the Bumblebee (Nikolai Rimsky-Korsakov)

The bumblebee is a black, yellow and white insect with a stout, hairy body. Like its smaller cousin, the honeybee, it eats pollen and nectar from flowers. It is a peaceful insect that rarely attacks humans. Only the female has a stinger. Scientists and engineers are mystified by the flight of the bumblebee, for it defies every law of aerodynamics. With wings too small for its body, this rather heavy insect shouldn't even be able to get off the ground. But it does! The music we selected here depicts the bumblebee's frenetic flying.

"Flight of the Bumblebee" is one of the best-known pieces from the classical repertoire. It is so fast and difficult that only performers of exceptional virtuosity dare attempt the solo arrangement. The original version is an orchestral interlude from the opera *The Tale of Tsar Saltan*, inspired by an Alexander Pushkin poem. It tells the story of young Prince Gvidon, sent into exile by his evil aunts when his father, the king, sets off to war. To help him regain his kingdom, a magical swan transforms the prince into an insect, at which point we hear the "Flight of the Bumblebee."

2 He spake the word, and there came all manner of flies...

Israel in Egypt (George Frideric Handel)

"He spake the word, and there came all manner of flies and lice in all quarters.

He spake; and the locusts came without number, and devoured the fruits of the ground."

Of all the insects, the fly is certainly best known to humans. It is found in every corner of the world, as far away as Antarctica. This creature is like a tiny robot with extra-sharp senses and extraordinary flying ability. Although flies don't bite, they can contaminate food by transmitting germs picked up from garbage. They feed primarily off spoiled food and decomposing animals. That is why a swarm of flies can be extremely harmful.

In his oratorio *Israel in Egypt*, Handel recounts the Biblical story of the ten plagues of Egypt, in which Yahweh sends a series of calamities upon the kingdom to convince the Pharaoh to free the Hebrew people held in slavery. One of the plagues is an infestation of flies.

3 From the Diary of a Fly

Mikrokosmos, Volume 6 (Béla Bartók)

The housefly has some unusual characteristics. For example, it can taste food with its legs: a fly can tell whether something is edible just by landing on it. Flies also have enormous eyes that see in every direction and sensitive hairs that can detect the movement of a nearby object (such as a fly swatter).

Béla Bartók knew of all these qualities as bugs fascinated him from a young age. As an adult, he kept an ordered and documented collection of insects. In this excerpt from Volume 6 of *Mikrokosmos*, "From the Diary of a Fly," Bartók uses the piano to help the listener imagine a series of events that make up a day in the life of a fly.

Bartók was interested in much more than music and insects. For example, he adored children and always took them very seriously. He composed 153 piano pieces for children in a series of books called *Mikrokosmos* (which means "small universe").

4 Overture

The Wasps, Aristophanic Suite
(Ralph Vaughan Williams)

The vast majority of wasps, recognized for their slender shape, furious buzzing and painful sting, are generally harmless to people. Quite to the contrary, they are beneficial in helping to control invasive insects. Maybe wasps owe their poor reputation to someone who had the misfortune of approaching a colony of wasps and was attacked by the swarm. A wasp is a social insect that is able to release pheromones to warn the nearby colony when it senses danger. The other wasps respond by preparing their stingers in a defensive reaction!

As a critique of the Athenian justice system, the Greek playwright Aristophanes drew inspiration from wasps for his play. The play's chorus members would dress as wasps, each with an enormous stinger. This piece represented jurors at an Athenian court (known for delivering stinging verdicts), hence the play's title: *The Wasps*.

Ralph Vaughan Williams wrote incidental music to *The Wasps* for a performance of Aristophanes's play in Cambridge. The music was so successful that, two years later, the composer decided to make an orchestral arrangement called an *Aristophanic Suite*.

5 The Night's Music

Out of Doors (Béla Bartók)

Summer nights in the country are a hurly-burly of sounds. Insects take advantage of the dark to search for food or to mate. While some are noticeable for their song (cicadas and crickets) or luminosity (fireflies), others, such as mites, beetles, roaches and moths, are more discrete. They all play an active role, however, in creating those familiar sounds of the night.

Out of Doors is the title of a suite of five pieces for piano. The fourth of these, called "The Night's Music," depicts the ambiance of nature at night by expressing peaceful energy. Later, the term "night music" would turn up in other music by Bartók in a similar style marked by a slow movement, mysterious dissonances, sounds imitating nature and solitary melodies.

Music of Insects, Frogs and Toads

6

The Child and the Spells (Maurice Ravel)

At night in the country or out of doors, the stillness, the silence and the darkness allow us to hear sounds that we often miss during the day when we are busy with activities and surrounded by visual and auditory stimuli. This is especially true with insects. Just as Bartók did in the last piece, Ravel creates here a world of insect sounds by depicting a nighttime scene in a garden.

The Child and the Spells (*L'enfant et les sortilèges*) is an opera for children. Its libretto written by Sidonie-Gabrielle Colette was first performed in 1925. The plot is unusual: as a punishment, his mother confined the child to his room until he finishes his homework. Annoyed and upset, the child begins to destroy everything out of spite, including a tea set, books and furniture. When night falls, the boy follows his cat out into the garden and again begins attacking everything at hand. At this point, as if by magic, the broken objects and animals come to life one by one to reproach the boy for his cruelty. Heeding them, he is finally remorseful.

7 The Frogs

Violin Concerto (Georg Philipp Telemann)

Yes, you're quite right: frogs—those funny little jumping green creatures with bulging eyes—are amphibians, not insects. Still, as "little creatures," they merit a place in this collection. Besides their legendary jumping, frogs are well known for croaking, a sound they produce with an air sac below their throat that acts as a resonance chamber. Frogs fill the sac with air and then gradually release it to produce a sound that can be more or less loud—one that you certainly have heard on a still summer evening. And while frogs enjoy wading in a pond, they prefer gathering together to croak. The resulting sound is unforgettable.

In this violin concerto, Telemann has created an amusing concert of frogs.

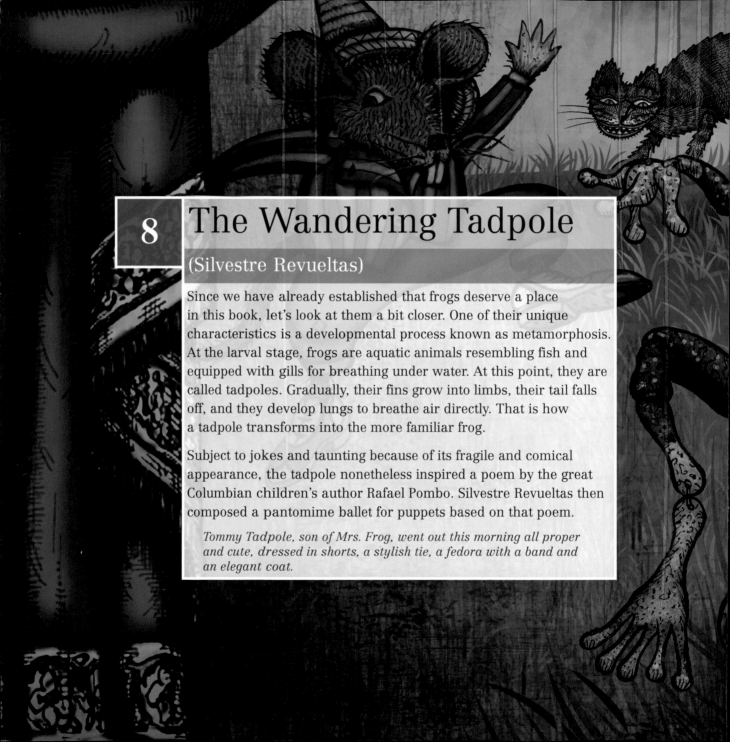

8 The Wandering Tadpole

(Silvestre Revueltas)

Since we have already established that frogs deserve a place in this book, let's look at them a bit closer. One of their unique characteristics is a developmental process known as metamorphosis. At the larval stage, frogs are aquatic animals resembling fish and equipped with gills for breathing under water. At this point, they are called tadpoles. Gradually, their fins grow into limbs, their tail falls off, and they develop lungs to breathe air directly. That is how a tadpole transforms into the more familiar frog.

Subject to jokes and taunting because of its fragile and comical appearance, the tadpole nonetheless inspired a poem by the great Columbian children's author Rafael Pombo. Silvestre Revueltas then composed a pantomime ballet for puppets based on that poem.

Tommy Tadpole, son of Mrs. Frog, went out this morning all proper and cute, dressed in shorts, a stylish tie, a fedora with a band and an elegant coat.

9

String Quartet opus 50, no. 6,

The Frog (Franz Joseph Haydn)

Frogs croak as a means of communication in various situations. Males, for example, croak to attract females, acknowledge the supremacy of another male, or warn other frogs of nearby danger.

Haydn's quartet opus 50, no. 6, is called *The Frog* because the fourth movement begins with a single note repeated several times alternately on two strings: an open string and the adjacent lower string. Known as bariolage, this technique creates a resonant sound reminiscent of frogs croaking.

10 The Cricket

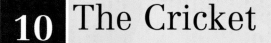

(Josquin des Prez)

Crickets are among people's favourite insects. These small jumping bugs are territorial animals. It is not unusual to see a cricket who has lost a leg or part of a wing to a rival. Crickets are renowned for their singing, which brightens a summer night in the country or a peaceful evening by a warm fireplace. Male crickets "sing" by rubbing their wings together in order to attract a female. Hence, crickets have long been associated with musicians and served as the main character in many tales and fables, such as *The Cricket and the Butterfly* and *The Cricket on the Hearth*. Other charming personifications of the cricket include Pinocchio's friend Jiminy Cricket and the cricket in the song you are about to hear.

The cricket is a good singer who holds long notes.
Go ahead cricket, drink and sing! But don't be like other birds,
who leave after they have sung a short while.
The cricket always holds his ground.
On the hottest day, he sings alone of love.

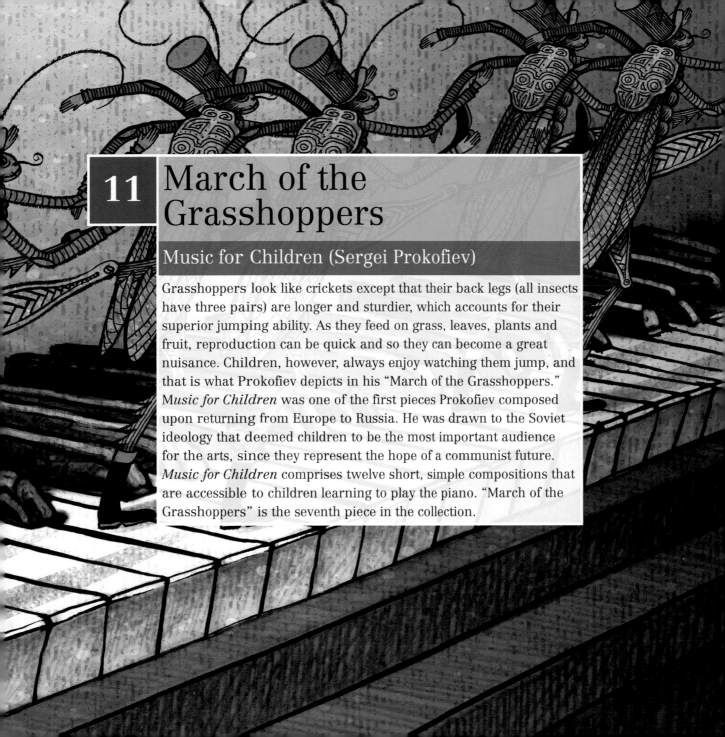

11 March of the Grasshoppers

Music for Children (Sergei Prokofiev)

Grasshoppers look like crickets except that their back legs (all insects have three pairs) are longer and sturdier, which accounts for their superior jumping ability. As they feed on grass, leaves, plants and fruit, reproduction can be quick and so they can become a great nuisance. Children, however, always enjoy watching them jump, and that is what Prokofiev depicts in his "March of the Grasshoppers." *Music for Children* was one of the first pieces Prokofiev composed upon returning from Europe to Russia. He was drawn to the Soviet ideology that deemed children to be the most important audience for the arts, since they represent the hope of a communist future. *Music for Children* comprises twelve short, simple compositions that are accessible to children learning to play the piano. "March of the Grasshoppers" is the seventh piece in the collection.

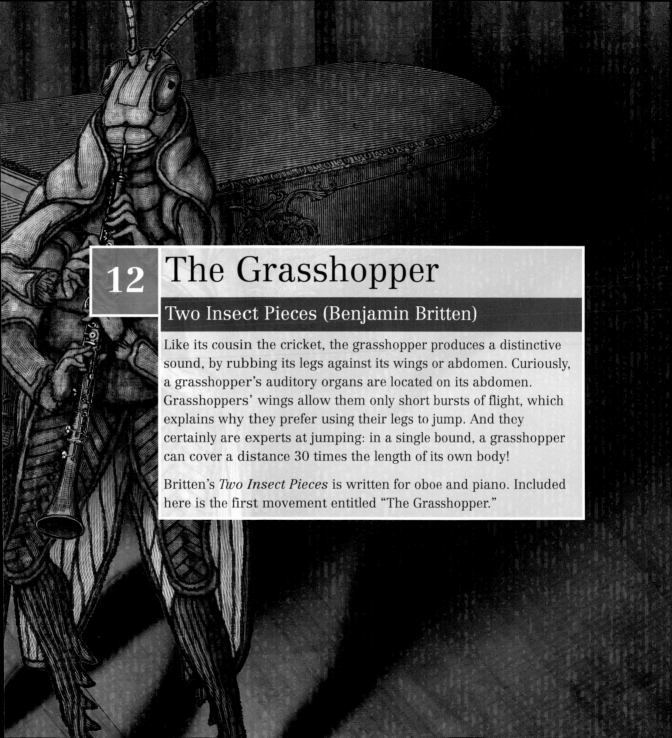

12 The Grasshopper

Two Insect Pieces (Benjamin Britten)

Like its cousin the cricket, the grasshopper produces a distinctive sound, by rubbing its legs against its wings or abdomen. Curiously, a grasshopper's auditory organs are located on its abdomen. Grasshoppers' wings allow them only short bursts of flight, which explains why they prefer using their legs to jump. And they certainly are experts at jumping: in a single bound, a grasshopper can cover a distance 30 times the length of its own body!

Britten's *Two Insect Pieces* is written for oboe and piano. Included here is the first movement entitled "The Grasshopper."

13 Song of the Flea

Goethe's *Faust* (Ludwig van Beethoven)

Dark-coloured fleas are tiny, wingless parasites that live hidden away in the fur or feathers of other animals. Their mouths include a tubal mechanism that they use to suck blood from their hosts. While the flea's bite generally causes itching, it also represents a far more ominous threat: fleas can transmit serious diseases such as typhus and the Black Death. It is safe to say that no one ever wants to have fleas! Nonetheless, the tiny flea's place in human cultural heritage far outweighs its size.

One such example is the "Song of the Flea," which appears in Johann Wolfgang von Goethe's *Faust*—one of the most celebrated works in all literature. Many composers have set this poem to music, including Beethoven.

A king there was once reigning,
Who had a goodly flea,
Him loved he without feigning,
As his own son were he!
His tailor then he summon'd,
The tailor to him goes;
Now measure me the youngster
For jerkin and for hose!

In satin and in velvet
Behold the younker dressed;
Bedizen'd o'er with ribbons,
A cross upon his breast.
Prime Minister they made him,
He wore a star of state;
And all his poor relations
Were courtiers, rich and great.

The gentlemen and ladies
at court were sore distressed;
The queen and all her maidens
Were bitten by the pest,
And yet they dared not scratch them,
Or chase the fleas away.
If we are bit, we catch them
And crack them without delay.

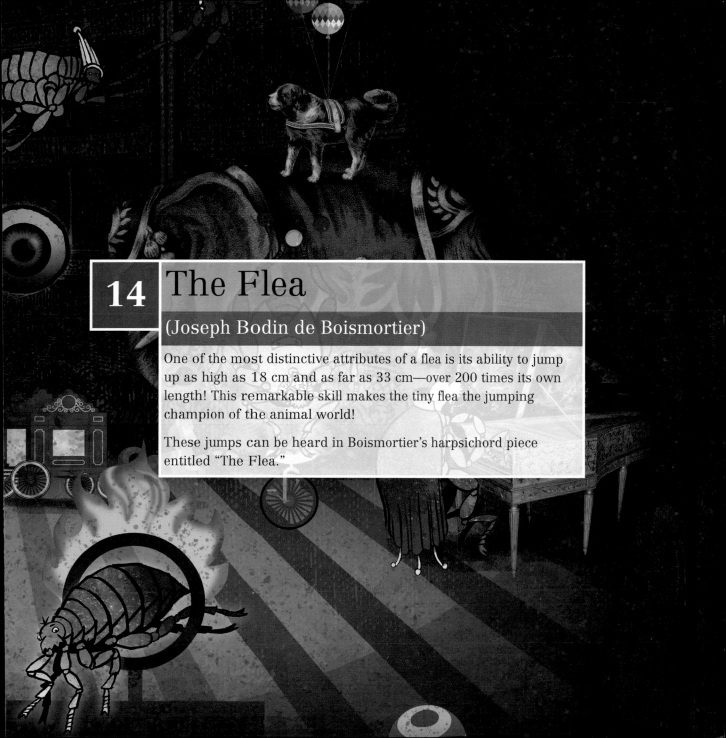

14 The Flea

(Joseph Bodin de Boismortier)

One of the most distinctive attributes of a flea is its ability to jump up as high as 18 cm and as far as 33 cm—over 200 times its own length! This remarkable skill makes the tiny flea the jumping champion of the animal world!

These jumps can be heard in Boismortier's harpsichord piece entitled "The Flea."

15 Tarantella

Bardic Sounds (Johann Kaspar Mertz)

Tarantulas are large, hairy spiders, usually black or brown in colour. Despite their terrifying appearance, they are not aggressive unless provoked. Their name comes from the city of Tarento in southern Italy, which also lends its name to the tarantella, a folk dance with links to the tarantula. According to legend, anyone unfortunate enough to be bitten by a tarantula was forced to dance for hours or even days to sweat away all of the spider's venom. This explains the dance's quick and rhythmic nature. The music is intended to drive dancers to move ever faster until not a drop of poison remains in their bodies.

Something about tarantellas drew many classical composers to write music inspired by this famous dance. One such piece is the sixth in *Bardic Sounds,* Mertz's best-known work.

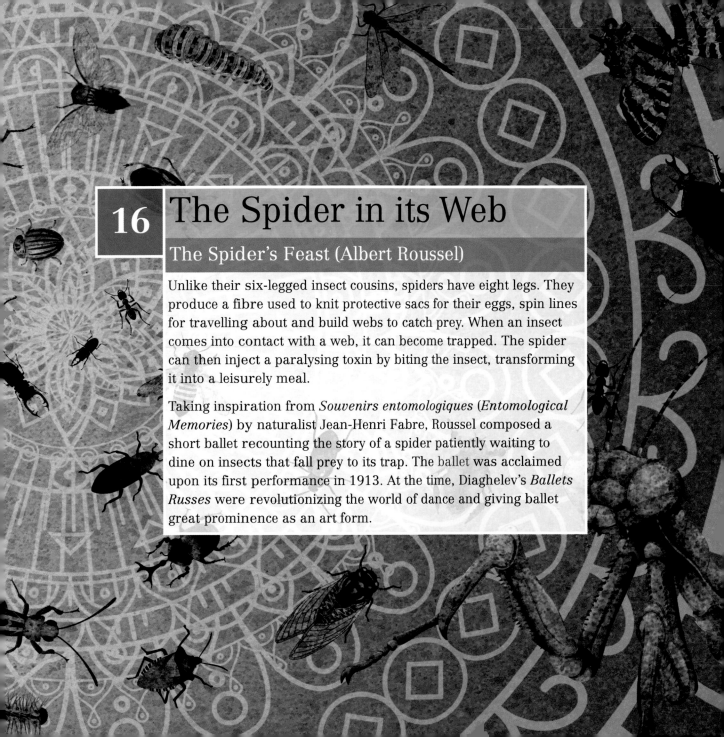

16 The Spider in its Web

The Spider's Feast (Albert Roussel)

Unlike their six-legged insect cousins, spiders have eight legs. They produce a fibre used to knit protective sacs for their eggs, spin lines for travelling about and build webs to catch prey. When an insect comes into contact with a web, it can become trapped. The spider can then inject a paralysing toxin by biting the insect, transforming it into a leisurely meal.

Taking inspiration from *Souvenirs entomologiques* (*Entomological Memories*) by naturalist Jean-Henri Fabre, Roussel composed a short ballet recounting the story of a spider patiently waiting to dine on insects that fall prey to its trap. The ballet was acclaimed upon its first performance in 1913. At the time, Diaghelev's *Ballets Russes* were revolutionizing the world of dance and giving ballet great prominence as an art form.

17 Entrance of the Ants

The Spider's Feast (Albert Roussel)

Ants live in organized colonies of up to eight million "citizens," each with a specific job to do. For example, leafcutter ants have large jaws that can cut a leaf into small pieces. Worker ants then line up in a row to transport those pieces on their back. Weaver ants build nests from leaf fragments. Each ant can carry up to 20 times its own weight (the equivalent for you of lifting a small car). Ants communicate with one another through chemical substances that warn of danger or point to a promising source of food. With all these attributes, ants are often held up in religious texts and children's fables as an example of hard work and cooperation.

In *The Spider's Feast*, ants are among the insects that parade before the web (strategically placed in the centre of the stage to catch the dancing insects). Organized in a single line, the ants have the incredible good fortune of not being captured by the spider.

18 The Butterflies

(François Couperin)

Among the varied species of insect, butterflies are the most poetic. With their many colours, lightness and fragility, they embody ideas of femininity, love, redemption of the soul and immortality. As well, the mutation from caterpillar to butterfly is truly remarkable.

In Couperin's piece entitled *The Butterflies* (*Les papillons*), the movement of the music illustrates some of these qualities.

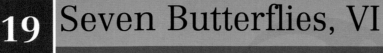

19 Seven Butterflies, VI

(Kaija Saariaho)

Kaija Saariaho once confided that the cello is her favourite instrument. She makes innovative use of it in her music, exploring its sonorous texture with the help of electronic resources and original performance techniques (varying the pressure or angle of the bow, for example). Such is the case in these seven miniatures that exploit the possibilities of the cello in depicting both the movement and the delicate, ephemeral nature of butterfly wings.

20 Sensemayá

(Silvestre Revueltas)

The nearly 3,000 species of snake come in a wide range of sizes and colours. Some 375 of those species are poisonous, while others, such as boas and pythons, kill their prey by constriction. Although many cultures have admired and even venerated these reptiles, some see them as representing danger and symbolizing evil, which explains why they are killed on sight without hesitation.

The poem *Sensemayá* by the Cuban author Nicolás Guillén describes a specific African rite:

Chant for Killing a Snake

Mayombe, bombe, mayombé!
Mayombe, bombe, mayombé!
Mayombe, bombe, mayombé!

The snake has eyes of glass;
it arrives and coils around a stick;
with eyes of glass, around a stick,
with eyes of glass.

The snake walks without legs;
it hides in the grass;
walking, it hides in the grass,
walking without legs.

Mayombe, bombe, mayombé!
Mayombe, bombe, mayombé!
Mayombe, bombe, mayombé!

Strike it with an axe and it dies:
go ahead, strike it now!
Don't kick it, it will bite you,
don't kick it, it will escape!

Sensemayá, the snake,
Sensemayá.

Drawn to the poem's musicality, Silvestre Revueltas used it as the basis for one of the most important compositions of the twentieth century.

Listening Guide

1 The Tale of Tsar Saltan

Flight of the Bumblebee (Nikolai Rimsky-Korsakov)
Bratislava Symphony Orchestra (CSR) / Conductor: Anthony Bramail

Playing multiple notes at breakneck speed, the strings imitate the buzzing of a bumblebee. The flute then takes over before the strings return to pick up the theme in a series of rapid crescendos and decrescendos, echoing the bumblebee's quick ability to move away and come back in close. In addition to the humming theme, a pizzicato melody lends a Russian flavour to this brilliant and colourful work.

2 He spake the word, and there came all manner of flies...

Israel in Egypt (George Frideric Handel)
Aradia Ensemble / Conductor: Kevin Mallon

Supported by brass, the male chorus solemnly proclaims what the Lord has said. This is contrasted by the women's chorus announcing the arrival of the flies, as the violins imitate their steady droning. This pattern is repeated twice, then the two elements are gradually combined—the solemn brass phrase over the buzzing violins and the voices of the men on top of those of the women—to portray the chaos generated by the infestation of flies.

3 From the Diary of a Fly

Mikrokosmos, Volume 6 (Béla Bartók)
Piano: Lajos Kertesz

Closely spaced, quiet notes on the piano create the image of a fly gently beginning its day. It gradually picks up energy when suddenly, to the sound of an ascending melody, it becomes entangled in a spider's web. The event is specified in the score. The piano produces many dissonant (see *dissonance* in the glossary), rhythmic and strident sounds that communicate the little creature's desperate anguish. Its fate is soon revealed: although nothing is written in the score, the music tells us that the fly has extricated itself and continues its buzzing without further incident.

4 Overture

The Wasps, Aristophanic Suite (Ralph Vaughan Williams)
Royal Liverpool Philharmonic / Conductor: James Judd

At the start of the overture, you will hear long, high woodwind trills imitating the buzzing of wasps. The strings soon take over in the middle register with rising and falling scales to depict the insects' frenetic movement. Other instruments join in, taking the trills even higher and lending an even more threatening character to the wasps' flight. When this reaches a peak, low woodwinds begin a joyful melody based on folk tunes that are soon taken up by the whole orchestra.

5 The Night's Music

Out of Doors (Béla Bartók)
Piano: Jen Jandó

The piece begins quietly to a regular beat marking groups of four very dissonant notes played together. Such groups are known as clusters. Bartók uses them to create a dark background against which one can hear at regular intervals high-pitched sounds evocative of nocturnal insects. The music establishes a strange atmosphere that is somehow both anxious and peaceful.

6   Music of Insects, Frogs and Toads

The Child and the Spells (Maurice Ravel)
Nashville Symphony / Conductor: Alastair Willis

To fully appreciate this piece, you need to open your ears wide to figure out the different sounds, similar to being in the country at night. Over soft tremolos in the strings, representing the muted humming of the insects, you will hear descending glissandos in a higher register played by an instrument rarely used in classical music: the slide whistle. The sound could be the hooting of an owl or the noise of some other nocturnal animal. Soon the song of a nightingale (a bird famous for singing at night) begins, followed by a choir that uses onomatopoeic sounds to imitate the croaking of frogs and toads.

7   The Frogs

Violin Concerto (Georg Philipp Telemann)
Ensemble Baroque ORFEO / Conductor and violin: Elizabeth Wallfisch

The concerto opens with a joyful melody played by the strings. The solo violin then enters, imitating the croaking of a frog. Another violin soon does likewise and then, gradually, more and more strings join in until the music sounds like a chorus of frogs after the rain has stopped. The melodic material returns later.

8   The Wandering Tadpole

(Silvestre Revueltas)
Simón Bolívar Symphony Orchestra / Conductor: Maximiano Validés

A timpani stroke and resonating cymbal follow a trumpet call announcing the prince's arrival. After several bass drum notes establish the rhythm, a trombone plays a melody that creates a fantastical scene in our imagination: a tadpole taking a brisk walk one fine morning. Listen carefully to the comical use of various musical resources, including brass colours, playful rhythms, dissonances and false notes—each used to tell the story of "The Wandering Tadpole."

9 String Quartet opus 50, no. 6,

The Frog (Franz Joseph Haydn)
Kodály Quartet

A famous author once said that when you listen to a string quartet you hear four intelligent people in conversation. Keep this image in mind as you listen to this piece. The first violin begins alone, playing the repeated note motif (bariolage). Given the movement's rapid tempo, it is difficult to make out the difference in timbre between the two strings, but you will notice the motive's distinct character. Does it remind you of frogs croaking? You'll have lots of opportunities to decide since the motive is repeated several times throughout the excerpt. In the second measure, as the first violin plays a series of different notes, the other three instruments imitate the original motive, repeating the note on just one string, however. Try to follow the four voices in conversation. You'll be impressed with the result!

10 The Cricket

(Josquin des Prez)
Capilla Flamenca

This piece is a frottola. While this sounds like a rather odd word, the piece is actually a very simple work for four voices that imitate the song of a cricket. You will notice that the music speeds up in the refrain to comic effect.

11 March of the Grasshoppers

Music for Children (Sergei Prokofiev)
Piano: Olli Mustonen

In the opening measures, you will hear a broken melody set to a walking rhythm that is suggestive of jumping grasshoppers. Almost immediately, the first phrase is inverted in a much lower register. Further on, a more flowing melody retains a bouncy nature by using the same rhythmic motive. Changes in register—a technique not often used in pieces for children—add colour while reinforcing the sense of jumping from one range to another every few seconds.

12 The Grasshopper

Two Insect Pieces (Benjamin Britten)
Oboe: Helen Jahren / Piano: Elizabeth Westenholz

The composer uses the instruments at his disposal to depict the two most distinctive characteristics of grasshoppers. Short, percussive notes in the piano represent jumping, while the higher sound of the oboe playing a more sustained line recalls the insect's song (although the oboe occasionally joins in with the piano for some jumping).

13 Song of the Flea

Goethe's Faust (Ludwig van Beethoven)
Baritone: Hermann Prey / Piano: Leonard Hokanson

The piano introduces a melody that alludes to the jumping flea. The bass soloist then recounts the humorous tale as the piano assumes an accompaniment role while still occasionally repeating the jumping motive. This piece is so simple that it might be mistaken for a popular song, but in reality, it is one of the earliest examples of a lied.

14 The Flea

(Joseph Bodin de Boismortier)
Harpsichord: Jacques Willemijms

One seldom hears the harpsichord nowadays, but 300 years ago it was a very popular instrument. Listen close to its delicate metallic timbre, admirably suited for depicting a flea. A melody formed of ever wider intervals always starting from the same note draws to mind a jumping flea. The melody is then repeated with variations.

15 Tarantella

Bardic Sounds (Johann Kaspar Mertz)
Guitar: Adam Holzman

In the opening measures of this piece, you will hear a short introduction that sets the rhythm and tonality while allowing the performer time to warm up their fingers. When the tarantella gets going, the lively, joyous melody will make you want to dance even if you haven't been bitten by a tarantula! The sound of the guitar perfectly captures the distinct nature of this popular dance.

16 The Spider in its Web

The Spider's Feast (Albert Roussel)
Royal Scottish National Orchestra / Conductor: Stéphane Denève

Unlike many other little creatures, spiders are silent. With no sounds to imitate, composers must be resourceful in helping us imagine a spider's patience and agility. At the start of this piece, we hear woodwinds play a calm melody in the middle register as the violins add a light touch above them. Descending chromatic motives soon depict the spider sliding down a web to test its strength.

17 Entrance of the Ants

The Spider's Feast (Albert Roussel)
Royal Scottish National Orchestra / Conductor: Stéphane Denève

The arrival of the ants is announced by ascending notes in the violins. Staccato notes in a high register suggest their small size and light steps, while a melody comprising a repeated fragment from the same rising phrase illustrates their disciplined nature. You will notice that these ideas are reinforced by a rhythmic march in the bassoons. At one point, the column of advancing ants is brought to a halt by a rose petal that falls across their path to threatening sounds from the brass section followed by a trill. As the ants decide to pick up the petal and carry it with them, a great heaviness in the music portrays the colossal effort deployed by the ants to lift their load. With the petal on their backs, the ants resume their agile, steady gait.

18 The Butterflies

(François Couperin)
Harpsichord: Christophe Rousset

As you listen to this piece, you will hear a continuous light, circular melody in the upper line interacting with a second lower melody that captures our attention. Notice a series of recurrent ornaments and a rhythmic motive that seems to give it more substance. Together, the melodies create the impression of two butterflies fluttering about.

19 Seven Butterflies, VI

(Kaija Saariaho)
Cello: Anssi Karttunen

You have heard the cello before, but probably never imagined that it could produce the kind of sounds you hear in this piece. Light taps on the fingerboard at the start of the piece, trills between real notes and harmonics, glissandi up and down, sounds produced by bow pressure—these elements feed the imagination with the light, continuous movement of a butterfly as expressed through a unique and hypnotic world of sound.

20 Sensemayá

(Silvestre Revueltas)
Mexico Festival Orchestra / Conductor: Enrique Bátiz

The work begins with the sound of a gong marking the start of the rite. Toms then establish a rhythm while the bass clarinet softly plays a repetitive line oscillating between two notes. An ostinato arises out of this undulating idea, producing a hypnotic effect and suggesting the presence of the snake. Eventually, the bassoon joins in with a circular melody that repeats every seven notes. You will also hear the sharp sound of claves struck together occasionally. Most of all, against this background, the snake's theme is played by the tuba surrounded by the mysterious aura of a ringing gong.

The Composers

Nikolai Rimsky-Korsakov (1844–1908)

Russian nationalist composer. Rimsky-Korsakov began playing piano at a very young age, displaying obvious artistic talent. He would go on to a brilliant career in the Russian navy, composing his first symphony at the age of 18 while aboard the military sailing ship *Almaz*. He continued to compose and teach music in parallel with his military career, first as an officer in the Russian Imperial Army, then as a civil inspector of naval bands. In 1861, he met Russian composer Mili Balakirev, who continually encouraged him to compose and introduced him to several young nationalist composers. The two friends would go on to form the Group of Five, an association of composers who drew inspiration from traditional Russian folksongs and employed harmonic, melodic and rhythmic elements unfamiliar to Western traditions.

George Frideric Handel (1685–1759)

German-born British composer. He is one of the most important musicians of the baroque period and of all time. Handel was an extraordinarily prolific musician whose work influenced all the styles of his time, even though he composed mainly operas and oratorios. Thanks to him, these two genres reached their golden age.

From a very young age, Handel showed tremendous talent, but his father, a court barber-surgeon, did not consider music a respectable profession and decided that his son would be a lawyer. It is said that a young George would sneak off to the attic at night to practice on a discarded harpsichord. It is also said that it was the Prince of Saxe, informed of the child's genius, who convinced the father to allow Handel to take formal lessons.

At age 17, Handel was already an organist at a church in his native town, but this position was not a good match for his tastes or ambition. Following study tours in Germany and Italy, he settled down in London in 1712; he would remain there for the rest of his life. *The Messiah,* composed in 1741 in only 24 days, is one of the most famous oratorios in the history of music.

Handel rests in the venerable Westminster Abbey.

Béla Bartók (1881–1945)

Of Hungarian origin, Bartók was one of the most important and original composers of the 20th century. He spent his childhood in a variety of Hungarian villages where his widowed mother was sent to teach. She would be his first piano teacher. At seventeen, Bartók went to live in Budapest, where he was admitted to the Franz Liszt Academy of Music. Later, he would embark on a journey through Hungary and Romania with composer friend Zoltán Kodály. During their travels, he collected thousands of melodies and songs that he recorded on a phonograph and transcribed into notebooks. Although he conducted exhaustive research and study of traditional folksongs, Bartók incorporated this material into his compositions only on rare occasions. He developed a personal style infused with great strength and marked by unusual melodic lines bounding in energy and accompanied by dissonant harmonies and asymmetrical syncopated rhythms typical of folk music found in the Balkans and Hungary.

He became a piano teacher and assistant director at the Academy of Music. In 1934, he left those positions to pursue research in grassroots musicology and perform piano recitals throughout Europe, all the while continuing to compose. The onset of World War II forced him to flee his homeland and take refuge in the United States. He died in New York at the age of 64, leaving an important heritage in every genre of classical music.

Ralph Vaughan Williams (1872–1958)

British composer and conductor known for his deep interest in English folklore and Renaissance music. It can be said that he was the leading English representative of musical nationalism during the first half of the 20th century.

Vaughan Williams composed an extensive body of work, which includes symphonies, piano concertos, orchestral and choral compositions, various song collections, operas and incidental music.

Williams died in London at 85. He rests in Westminster Abbey, near the famous English composer Sir Henry Purcell.

Maurice Ravel (1875–1937)

Ravel had a happy childhood, enjoying the attention of cultured parents who encouraged him to develop his musical talent. At six, he began learning the piano and, at 14, he entered the Conservatoire de Paris where he studied composition with Gabriel Fauré. In 1905, Ravel failed to win the highly coveted Prix de Rome for the fifth time (his music being deemed too radical in traditional circles). Closely followed by the press, the incident provoked a scandal in the musical community and stirred a wave of sympathy for the audacious young composer that resonated beyond the borders of France. Around this time, distinct characteristics of his music began to emerge: a particular taste for the supernatural and the exotic, as well as for Spanish and Oriental sonorities, but especially a melodic refinement and formal perfection that were the result of his legendary meticulous craftsmanship. More than just a talented composer, Maurice Ravel was an excellent conductor with a reputation for working with orchestral timbres to create a harmonious balance among the instruments. His brilliant orchestrations gave many works originally written for piano a whole new dimension.

Georg Philipp Telemann (1681–1767)

German composer. A contemporary and acquaintance of Bach and Handel, Telemann is considered to be a bridge between the Baroque and Classical periods.

At the age of ten, Telemann displayed an interest in music and proved to be quite talented. Despite his widowed mother's efforts to discourage him, Telemann continued to compose and to develop his musical skills on his own, with the support of his school principal. He learned to play the organ, violin, flute and oboe almost without assistance. He began legal studies at Leipzig University when he was 20, but soon gave those up when his considerable musical talent was recognised. Telemann received commissions to compose religious music for the city's main churches. Shortly thereafter, he was appointed director of the Leipzig Opera. This was the start of an illustrious musical career in which he held several prestigious positions and was able to dedicate himself to composing music of all types. He went on to direct the Hamburg Opera and travel throughout Germany. Telemann was a prolific composer in all the musical forms of his time: operas and cantatas as well as orchestral and chamber compositions. He was also an impresario, publisher and very active author. In all these roles, he was able to bring music to the common people when it had hitherto been the exclusive domain of the Church, court or city.

Silvestre Revueltas (1899–1940)

Revueltas showed musical talent from a very young age. He was given his first violin when he was seven, and by the time he was eight, he had formed an ensemble with other children whom he reportedly paid with candy. When he was 14, his father sent him to Mexico's National Conservatory of Music where he studied for three years. The following year, he moved to the United States to complete his training, obtaining a degree in violin and composition from the Chicago College of Music. During the 1920s and 1930s, he worked to introduce concert music throughout Mexico, serving as assistant conductor of the newly formed National Symphonic Orchestra and director of the League of Revolutionary Writers and Artists. Moved by his political convictions, Revueltas visited Spain in the midst of the Spanish Civil War in support of the Republican cause. Back in Mexico, he composed many symphonic works while continuing to teach.

Silvestre Revueltas was one of a group of nationalist composers striving to renew their art form by restoring values associated with the music of indigenous peoples and pre-Hispanic times, while growing closer to the European avant-garde movement. Revueltas exploited instrumental resources to the fullest, handling strings like percussion instruments and giving brass a melodic accent reminiscent of town bands. His musical language is tonal with a certain degree of dissonance, displaying great rhythmic vitality and often with a distinct Mexican flavour. He is considered to be Mexico's most influential composer because of the scope and originality of his music.

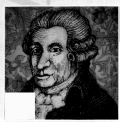

Franz Joseph Haydn (1732–1809)

A prolific Austrian composer who, together with Mozart and Beethoven, was the leading embodiment of the Classical period. The son of a village wheelwright, he became familiar with the folk music of local Croatian peasants as a young child. Gifted with a beautiful voice, at eight he became a chorister at St. Stephen's Cathedral in Vienna, where he developed his musical skills. When his voice changed at 17, he was dismissed from the choir and had to earn a living as an independent musician. During this difficult period, he held several positions: music teacher, serenade singer, secretary and accompanist to Italian composer Nicola Porpora. This was when he began to compose, and his music soon attracted the attention of the Austrian aristocracy. In 1761, he entered the service of one of the era's wealthiest and most influential families, the Esterházys. The new position placed at his disposal one of Europe's best orchestras, for which he would write most of his orchestral works, religious music and operas. He remained in the employ of the Esterházy family for thirty years, building an international reputation, especially for his symphonies and quartets (a form he pioneered).

His innovative ability to transform a motif or simple melody into complex musical developments fascinated his contemporaries. His style is marked by sudden dramatic changes that create surprising humoristic effects.

Josquin des Prez (c. 1450–1521)

Franco-Flemish composer. Highly respected during his lifetime, Josquin is considered one of the most important Renaissance composers. Contemporaries nicknamed him the "prince" of musicians, and copyists attributed anonymous works to his name to increase sales. Martin Luther wrote of him: "He is the master of the notes. They must do as he wills; as for the other composers, they have to do as the notes will."

Little is known, however, of his life. Believed to have been born in the County of Hainaut (today part of Belgium), he was a disciple of Johannes Ockeghem, a great composer in the Franco-Flemish School. A singer at the Milan Cathedral, Josquin later entered into service at the papal chapel in Rome before moving on to Florence, Modena and Ferrara. In 1509, he returned to his native country, where he became provost of the collegiate church of Notre-Dame in Condé-sur-l'Escaut.

His extensive output includes masses, motets and polyphonic songs. His music is characterised by an expressive treatment of text that reflects the humanist ideals of the time, as opposed to more abstract earlier styles that often ignored the meaning of words.

Sergueï Prokofiev (1891–1956)

Twentieth century Russian composer. A child prodigy, he received his first music lessons from his mother, an amateur pianist. He composed his first opera, *The Giant,* at age nine. At 13, he entered the Saint Petersburg Conservatory (he remains the youngest student in the conservatory's history), where he took an interest in the most avant-garde trends of the time. His first works, which were dissonant and deliberately raucous, earned him a reputation as an ultramodern musician. Following the October 1917 revolution, and in search of peace, for composing more than for ideological reasons, Prokofiev left the USSR and settled in the West. In 1933, after 15 years of exile, nostalgia led him to return and settle in his country.

In Soviet Russia, all artistic creations had to respect the dogmas of socialist realism. As a result, some of Prokofiev's works were considered too modern and were prohibited. He therefore adopted a more classical style, and the melodic element of his compositions became more prominent. Some of his best-known works are from this time: the children's tale *Peter and the Wolf,* as well as the ballets *Romeo and Juliet* and *Cinderella*. Sergueï Prokofiev passed away on March 5, 1953, the same day as Joseph Stalin.

Benjamin Britten (1913–1976)

Pianist and conductor, Benjamin Britten was perhaps the most celebrated British composer of the twentieth century. Born November 22 (Saint Cecilia Day in honour of the patroness of musicians), Britten began playing the piano and composing at a very young age. After completing studies at the Royal College of Music, he began earning a living by writing music for the theatre, radio and film, immediately drawing public attention to his music. A dedicated pacifist, Britten decided to move to the United States as an expression of protest when the Second World War broke out. He returned to England in 1942, and in 1945 his first opera, Peter Grimes, brought him immediate international recognition. He now dedicated himself entirely to reinvigorating opera in his homeland.

In 1947, he founded the English Opera Group near the Royal Opera House (also known as Covent Garden); the following year he launched an annual music festival in Aldeburgh (where he would later live out his life) whose programming would make it one of Europe's most important events of its type. His prolific output covers every type of music: large forms and small, from simple songs to the imposing War Requiem (one of the most moving oratorios of modern time describing the unimaginable horrors of the Second World War), instrumental music and opera. Britten was the first English musician ever to be appointed a life peer.

Ludwig van Beethoven (1770–1827)

The son and grandson of musicians, Beethoven showed exceptional musical talent from an early age. Wanting the young Ludwig to follow in the steps of Mozart, his father soon began teaching him piano, organ and clarinet. At 14, Beethoven was appointed organist of the court chapel in his hometown. Three years later, Archduke Maximilian Franz of Austria sent him to Vienna to study with Mozart. For many reasons, Beethoven remained in Vienna but a short time and met Mozart on just one occasion. It is said that after hearing Beethoven play one of his pieces, Mozart commented, "Mark that young man; he will make himself a name in the world!"

In 1792, one year after Mozart had died, Beethoven made Vienna his home, studying composition with Joseph Haydn and Antonio Salieri. A quick learner, he soon gained a reputation in elite circles as a composer and pianist. When he was 25, Beethoven experienced hearing difficulties that would leave him deaf and unable to perform or conduct in public. Despite this handicap, he continued to compose magnificent music. He died at 57, leaving an immense musical heritage. Today he is considered one of the greatest composers of all time.

Joseph Bodin de Boismortier (1689–1755)

French flutist and composer of the Baroque period. He was born in Lorraine, where he spent his childhood and teenage years. Little is known about his musical education. In 1713, perhaps to avoid becoming a confectioner like his father, he moved to Perpignan and worked as a tax collector. Ten years later, he settled in Paris, where he quickly established his reputation as a composer. His works for voice and various combinations of instruments, often including the flute, had such popular appeal that he was able to earn a considerable income. It is said Boismortier was the first musician to earn a good living from his compositions.

Johann Kaspar Mertz (1806–1856)

Austro-Hungarian guitarist and composer of the Romantic period. He was born into a modest family in Pressburg (now Bratislava). Little is known of his childhood, but it is recorded that he was a flute and guitar prodigy. From 1840 until his death, Mertz lived in Vienna, home to other notable guitarists such as Anton Diabelli and Mauro Giuliani. There, he established a reputation as a guitar virtuoso. He performed major tours of Europe and married the concert pianist Joséphine Plantin. It is thought that the characteristic sound of his later compositions and unique right-hand technique derive from his close relationship with the piano. His guitar music, unlike that of his contemporaries, is modelled on the piano compositions of Chopin, Mendelssohn, Schubert and Schumann. Shortly after his death, he was awarded a prize at a major international competition for classical guitar composers.

Albert Roussel (1869–1937)

French composer. Although he began musical studies at a young age, these were only a complementary part of his education. At 18, he was admitted to the French naval academy and would remain with the navy for seven years. During that time, he made several voyages to Southeast Asia. The exotic discoveries he made there would later have a major influence on his dramatic and orchestral works. Deciding to dedicate his life to composition, Roussel left the navy when he was 25 and was accepted at the Schola Cantorum de Paris, where he went on to study with Vincent d'Indy and teach composition from 1902 to 1914. He had significant influence as a composition teacher, working with such notable students as Erik Satie and Edgard Varèse. During the First World War, he was sent to the front with the Red Cross, an experience that affected his health and forced him to retire to Brittany in 1918. From that point on, he dedicated himself solely to composition. Together with Debussy and Ravel, he is considered one of the most influential French musicians of the first half of the twentieth century.

François Couperin (1668–1733)

French composer, organist and harpsichordist. Nicknamed "Couperin the Great" by his contemporaries, he was one of the most important French composers of the Baroque period. He was born into and learned his craft from a long line of musicians who had distinguished themselves beyond two centuries. At 17, he became organist of the Church of Saint-Gervais de Paris, a position traditionally held by a member of his family. His skill as a performer facilitated entry into the court as organist of the Royal Chapel of Louis XIV, where he was charged with the musical education of the crown prince.

He composed sacred works and chamber music for the king and his courtiers, but his most important compositions are some 200 pieces for harpsichord: short descriptive pieces with suggestive titles in an elegant, refined and formal style. His treatise entitled L'art de toucher le clavecin [The Art of Harpsichord Playing] was held in high esteem by Johann Sebastian Bach. It explains harpsichord technique, fingering and ornaments and is considered an indispensable guide to understanding the Baroque style.

Kaija Saariaho (1952–)

Major Finnish composer. Born in Helsinki into a non-musical family, Saariaho explains that she developed great musical awareness in childhood. She listened to an old radio and heard music in her head, imagining it came from her pillow. When the music kept her from sleeping at night, she would even go and ask her mother to turn off the pillow. At six, she began to learn violin, piano and organ. She entered the Sibelius Academy as a composition student when she was 24. From there, she continued studies in Freiburg and then, in 1982, following her interest in electronic music, joined the Institute for Research and Coordination in Acoustics/Music (IRCAM) in Paris, where she lives to this day.

Saariaho has received numerous prestigious international awards. In 2008, she was named Musician of the Year for being "among the few contemporary composers to achieve public acclaim as well as universal critical respect." Her compositions, which combine acoustic and electronic music, are distinguished by rich, mysterious textures and are performed at major concert venues around the world.

Glossary of Musical Terms

Accompaniment: Musical background in support of a melody.

Arpeggio: Notes of a chord sounded rapidly in succession.

Ballet: Musical composition intended to accompany a staged dance performance.

Bariolage: String instrument technique involving a rapid alternation between a fixed note and changing notes that may be higher or lower than the fixed note. This technique is found frequently in Baroque music for the violin with the fixed note played on an open string and the changing notes on an adjacent string.

Bass: The lowest human voice or the low register of an instrument.

Bassoon: Woodwind instrument in the double-reed family, considered the bass of the oboe family.

Bow: Narrow stick of wood that is curved or folded at the ends and along which horsehair is stretched. The hairs are used to produce sound when drawn across the strings of certain musical instruments.

Brass: A family of resonant wind instruments that includes the trumpet, the French horn, the trombone and the tuba.

Cello: String instrument of the violin family whose size and register lie between those of the viola and the double bass. The cello is held between the knees and the strings are played with a bow. Many consider it to be the string instrument that most resembles the human voice. The cello has been a popular instrument with composers throughout music history because of its warm tone, versatility and expressive qualities.

Chorus (or choir): Ensemble of singers performing a musical composition.

Chord: Simultaneous sounding of three or more notes to produce a certain harmonic colour.

Chromatic: Adjective denoting a series of consecutive semitones.

Clarinet: Black woodwind instrument. Its timbre is rich in nuance and expressive possibilities. It is the most nimble instrument of the orchestra, after the flute, as well as one of the most versatile.

Claves: Common Latin-American percussion instrument in the form of two cylindrical sticks made of hardwood.

Cluster: Chord comprising a series of consecutive semitones (e.g., C, C#, D, D#, E and F) played at the same time.

Concerto: Composition in which a solo instrument has a dialogue with a group of instruments (the orchestra). The solo instrument (the soloist) plays the melody while the orchestra plays the accompaniment. These compositions, which appeared in the baroque period, are divided into three parts (movements). Generally, the first movement is quite fast, the second, a little slow, and the last movement is even faster than the first.

Cymbal: Percussion instrument consisting of two round bronze plates with a concave basin in the middle and flat edges. A leather loop is passed through a hole drilled in the centre to serve as a handle.

Dissonance: Combination of intervals that produces a disturbing sonority or creates tension.

Electronic: Musical genre that employs sounds produced by electronic devices such as synthesizers, samplers or computers.

False note: A deliberately incorrect note sung or played on an instrument.

Fingerboard: Piece of wood on a string instrument covering the neck, where the fingers are placed to obtain the desired notes.

Flute: Wind instrument. The simple design of the flute suggests that it may be the oldest of musical instruments. In one form or another, the flute is found in almost every known culture.

Frottola: Fifteenth-century composition for three or four voices in which the upper voice sings the melody. It has a simple form, employs clear, repetitive rhythms, and is of limited range. Frottolas may have an instrumental accompaniment.

Glissando (Italian term from the French *glisser*, "to slide"): Rapid execution of a scale toward the highest note (ascending) or the lowest (descending). In keyboard instruments such as the piano, the back of the hand is made to slide across the white keys.

Gong: Percussion instrument that originated in China. It is a large, circular metal disc, usually made of bronze, with the edges curved inwards. The gong is hung vertically and struck with a mallet.

Guitar: Plucked string instrument consisting of a wooden sound box with a circular hole and fretted neck.

Harmonic: Within the complex sound of a single note, a secondary sound of a higher frequency occurring simultaneously with the fundamental pitch of a lower frequency.

Harpsichord: Keyboard instrument widely used in the Baroque period. Contrary to the piano, the harpsichord has a string mechanism that is plucked using a plectrum, which produces a soft, slightly metallic sound more resembling that of a harp or guitar. Many pieces written for this instrument are now performed on the piano.

Interlude: Short instrumental composition performed between two sections of a larger work.

Lied (from the German *lied*, "song," lieder in the plural): Short vocal composition accompanied on the piano, of folk origin with a poetic touch. Well suited to the expression of emotions, this genre flourished during the Romantic period. The lied is characterized by brevity, relinquishing virtuosity and close relationship to poetry. The melody and accompaniment aim to translate the words of the poem into musical elements.

Low register: Set of notes of relatively low frequency.

Mass: Series of musical settings of texts from the Catholic mass (hence the term) intended for performance during a service.

Measure: Rhythmic division of a musical piece into equal parts.

Melody: Succession of different notes with a particular rhythm expressing a musical idea.

Motet: Short religious piece composed for several voices and generally performed in church. It was one of the most important musical forms from the thirteenth to the seventeenth centuries.

Motif: Short melodic or rhythmic idea that is the primary unit of a musical fragment.

Movement: One complete section (i.e. with a beginning and an end) of a composite work performed in succession with other such single pieces.

Note: Musical symbol that represents a sound. The term is often used for the sound itself.

Open string: Term to describe when a string instrument is played without the string being stopped by a finger.

Opera: Classical music genre that began in Italy at the end of the Renaissance and at the beginning of the Baroque period (1600). It is defined as a "theatrical piece put to music." The dialogues are sung and accompanied by an orchestra.

Oratorio: Dramatic lyrical composition dealing with sacred topics, with choir and orchestra.

Orchestra: Large group of musicians playing together. The actual size of the ensemble varies with the type of music performed.

Ostinato (from the Latin *obstinatus,* "obstinate"): A musical motive or phrase that is constantly repeated.

Overture: An instrumental composition that serves to introduce a larger work such as an opera by presenting the themes to follow. The overture to Mendelssohn's *A Midsummer Night's Dream* was the first truly independent overture intended for performance as a concert piece.

Percussion: Family of musical instruments (the oldest known) that produce sound when struck. The many types of percussion instruments are organized into two categories: instruments producing a definite pitch for playing specific notes (timpani, xylophone, vibraphone, tubular bells, etc.) and instruments of indefinite pitch (such as the bass drum, triangle, cymbal, tenor drum, etc.)

Pianissimo: Italian term used in music to indicate the lowest sound intensity; very softly.

Piano: Keyboard string instrument invented around 1700. Pressing a key causes a hammer to strike the corresponding string and produce a sound. The word piano is an abbreviation of pianoforte (from the Italian piano, "quiet," and forte, "loud"), which refers to the piano's ability to produce sounds of different intensities depending on the force applied to the keys, something which was not possible with its predecessors (the harpsichord and the clavichord), which could only produce one volume. The piano is the most significant instrument of Western music. In addition to the immense quantity of works composed for the piano and all its expressive possibilities (it is the instrument that can produce the most sounds at the same time), the piano is an essential element in the study of basic musical knowledge. It is an irreplaceable tool in the composition process.

Polyphonic song: Musical genre, generally for four mixed voices, that is typical of the French Renaissance and rooted in secular vocal music of the Middle Ages.

Phrase: A section of a melodic line forming a complete idea.

Quartet: Musical ensemble comprising four instruments or voices, or a piece written for performance by four instruments or voices. The string quartet, composed of two violins, viola and cello, was common in the Classical period and is considered one of the most significant chamber music formations.

Register: Range of a voice or instrument (from the highest pitch to the lowest).

Rhythm: The distribution of notes and rests in time.

Scale: Series of sounds produced in ascending or descending order. The most widely known scale is "do-re-mi-fa-so-la-ti-do."

Score: Transcription of the notes of a musical work.

Slide whistle: Instrument related to the recorder that uses a slide to vary the length of the column rather than holes to produce different notes. The slide is used to play distinctive ascending and descending glissandi. It is often used to create comical effects in film music.

Snare drum: Percussion instrument of indefinite pitch, usually with a shallow barrel. The distinctive timbre comes from a series of wires stretched under the lower skin, giving the drum a sound that is more strident and metallic than standard drums.

Soloist: A musician or instrument assigned a solo role (also see concerto).

Spiccato: String instrument technique that involves bouncing the bow slightly off the string.

Staccato (from the Latin *staccare,* "to detach"): Style of musical performance in which the length of a note is shortened from the notated value.

Strings: Family of instruments that produce sounds from vibrating strings. In the context of an orchestra, the string section includes violins, violas, cellos and double basses.

Suite: Instrumental composition made up of a series of short sections or movements. The suite, which appeared in the 16th century, includes a series of folk songs and dances generally in the same key. While they are all separate pieces, these songs and dances nevertheless combine to present strong contrasts between slow and fast tempos as well as majestic and cheerful modes. Today, the suite is simply a work made up of a series of short pieces with a common element.

Texture: Result of the interaction of various melodic lines in a piece of music.

Theme: The main idea, usually a recognizable melody, on which a composition is based in whole or in part.

Timbre: The sound quality that distinguishes two instruments or voices from one another, even when producing the same note.

Timpani (or kettledrum): The most important percussion instrument in the orchestra comprising a skin stretched over a hollow copper shell. The tension in the skin (and therefore the pitch) can be adjusted by screws or a pedal. Orchestral works usually call for two or three timpani, each assigned a different note.

Tom: Percussion instrument with an upper and a lower skin stretched over a cylindrical barrel about 20 cm to 25 cm in diameter. It is mounted on three legs, and the skin tension is regulated by adjusting screws and wires. Although they may be used alone, toms are usually found in sets of three. They are generally less resonant than other drums.

Tonality: The relationship between the different tones or musical notes.

Tremolo: The rapid repetition of a single note. While this technique can be used by any instrument, it is primarily associated with the strings.

Trill: A melodic ornament performed by rapidly and regularly alternating two pitches a whole tone or semitone apart.

Trombone: Wind instrument consisting of a long U-shaped metal tube with a slide to change the length and produce different notes. One end opens into a large bell. The clear, solemn sound of the trombone is pitched lower than the trumpet so that the two instruments are complementary.

Trumpet: Wind instrument made from a long metal tube of expanding diameter from the mouthpiece to the bell. The trumpet has a bright military sound and is equipped with efficient valves capable of fingering rapid passages.

Tuba: Largest member of the brass family of instruments, having a loud, deep sound.

Viola: String instrument similar to the violin, but slightly larger and lower in pitch.

Violin: Smallest member of the string family and one of the most popular instruments. Its beautiful tone and impressive richness of expression make the violin an ideal solo instrument that has been treasured by musicians and music lovers for centuries. Together with the larger and deeper sounding members of its family, it also plays a leading role at the heart of the orchestra. The violin is played by drawing a bow across its strings. It can also be played by plucking strings with a finger to produce a sound called pizzicato. Dating back to 1550, the violin is a descendant of the larger and deeper sounding viol family (*viola d'amore, viola da gamba*). On the surface, the violin is one of the simplest of modern instruments, comprising only a varnished wood sound box, a long neck and four taut strings. Appearances can deceive however: it takes some 70 pieces to build a violin!

Virtuosity: Technical ability of the instrumentalist.

Voice: Sound produced by the human vocal chords. In music, voice also refers to a specific melodic line played by any one instrument.

Wind instruments: Family of instruments that produce sounds when a musician blows into them. This large family comprises two groups: woodwinds (flute, oboe, clarinet and bassoon) and brass (trumpet, horn, trombone and tuba).

Woodwinds: Group of wind instruments that includes the flute, oboe, English horn, clarinet and bassoon. The other group of wind instruments is the brass, whose sound is louder and brighter.

Timeline of composers and periods

	1450	1500	1550
Josquin des Prez (v. 1450–1521)	▓	▓	
François Couperin (1668–1733)			
Georg Philipp Telemann (1681–1767)			
George Frideric Handel (1685–1759)			
Joseph Bodin de Boismortier (1689–1755)			
Franz Joseph Haydn (1732–1809)			
Ludwig van Beethoven (1770–1827)			
Johann Kaspar Mertz (1806–1856)			
Nikolai Rimsky-Korsakov (1844–1908)			
Albert Roussel (1869–1937)			
Ralph Vaughan Williams (1872–1958)			
Maurice Ravel (1875–1937)			
Béla Bartók (1881–1945)			
Sergueï Prokofiev (1891–1956)			
Silvestre Revueltas (1899–1940)			
Benjamin Britten (1913–1976)			
Kaija Saariaho (1952–)			

Renaissance

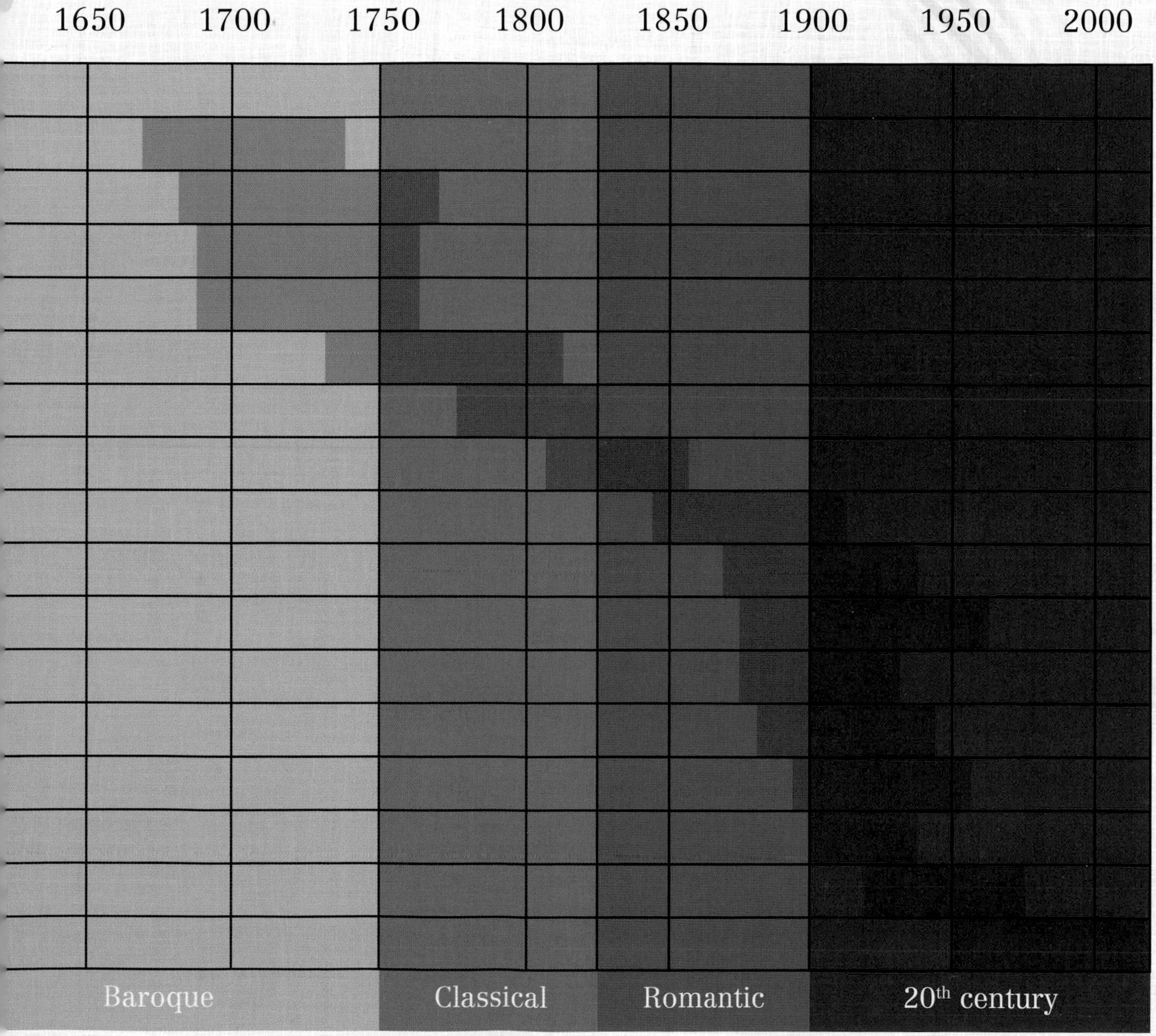
1650
1700
1750
1800
1850
1900
1950
2000
Baroque
Classical
Romantic
20th century

Music selection and explanatory notes Ana Gerhard

Illustrations Mauricio Gómez Morin

Translation from Spanish to English Les Services d'édition Guy Connolly

Graphic design Mora Diez and Stéphan Lorti

Publisher of original publication Daniel Goldin

Copy editing Ruth Joseph

First published in Spanish as *Bichos - Introducción a la música de concierto*

© 2018 Ana Gerhard (text), © 2018 Mauricio Gómez Morin (illustrations), 2018

© Editorial Océano / Master recordings under license from Libermex S. A de C.V.

�ⓦ www.thesecretmountain.com

●🅟 2019 The Secret Mountain (Folle Avoine Productions)

ISBN 13: 978-2-924774-55-7/ ISBN 10: 2-924774-55-1